A Walk Thru the Book of

LUKE

A Savior for the World

Walk Thru the Bible

BakerBooks

a division of Baker Publishing Group
Grand Rapids, Michigan

Published by Baker Books
a division of Baker Publishing Group
P.O. Box 6287, Grand Rapids, MI 49516-6287
www.bakerbooks.com

Printed in the United States of America

Library of Congress Cataloging-in-Publication Data
A walk thru the book of Luke : a Savior for the world / Walk Thru the Bible.
     p.   cm. — (Walk Thru the Bible discussion guides)
Includes bibliographical references.
ISBN 978-0-8010-7182-9 (pbk.)
1. Bible. N.T. Luke—Criticism, interpretation, etc. I. Walk Thru the Bible (Educational ministry).
BS2595.52.W35 2010
226.4007—dc22   2009053560

Scripture is taken from the HOLY BIBLE, NEW INTERNATIONAL VERSION®. NIV®. Copyright © 1973, 1978, 1984 by International Bible Society. Used by permission of Zondervan. All rights reserved.

10   11   12   13   14   15   16   7   6   5   4   3   2   1

Contents

Introduction

There was no shortage of religious options. Egyptian civilization had risen and fallen—several times, actually—and its religion influenced much of the world with its gods of nature and its complex descriptions of the afterlife. Babylonian and Persian religions did the same. Greek mythology offered its diverse pantheon, and Greek philosophers had cultivated sophisticated arguments for why and how things exist. Roman religion added ample choices to the spectrum too. By the time of the New Testament, the array of beliefs and mystery cults and philosophies and specialized deities was truly dizzying. People could jump from one belief to another, seeking whatever fit their personal tastes, and never run out of choices.

Israel's faith had never tolerated such diversity well—at least in those times when Israel was actually faithful. Its God was determined to be worshiped above all other gods. His power was displayed in ways that other gods never matched, and his desire for a devoted people was unparalleled in the ancient world. His character, too, was unique—a God who valued love, mercy, and righteousness above slavish service and sacrifices. He was a global God, at least theoretically. According to his

Word, he claimed worldwide authority and a desire for all to know him.

A man named Jesus stepped into this world with an unparalleled message. He came in the name of the God of Israel; he even claimed divine origin for himself. There were plenty of rival messiahs in the years before and after Jesus, but none demonstrated the kind of authority that the Nazarene commanded. He was the fulfillment of Israel's prophecies and hopes. He was the visible expression of the invisible God.

Though Luke presented Jesus as Israel's Messiah, he made it clear that Jesus was also the Savior of the world. This Savior did not come in the name of some local deity; he came for everyone who believes—for the weak and helpless, the diseased and destitute, the poor and needy, the sinful and outcast members of society, the Jews and Gentiles of all nations. He is never portrayed in any Gospel, including Luke's, as one more option on the spiritual buffet. Rather, he is hailed as the King of the coming kingdom. As such, he is someone a vast empire with hodgepodge beliefs should pay attention to.

The religious scene isn't all that different today than it was in Jesus's time. Melting-pot cultures and societies drawn closer by global communication offer a wide range of beliefs to suit anyone's desires. There are gods and goddesses, philosophies and practices, prayers and promises for all types of people and preferences—and a highly valued virtue called "tolerance" to protect such pluralism from the claims of exclusive religions. We live in a time where seeking truth is considered admirable but finding it is considered narrow-minded.

That's why the Gospel of Luke speaks to our generation as clearly as it spoke to the generation in which it was written. Jesus is not simply an addition to the religious landscape; he's the Lord of all creation. His powerful works back up his words, and his words call for a response. And that's Luke's purpose in writing: to urge a response. He gives a thorough account of the unique Son of God so that people in a diverse world will know the truth.

Themes

Luke seems intent on demonstrating that Jesus is the fulfillment of God's promises and prophecies from ages past. God has had a plan from the very beginning and has faithfully carried out that plan throughout the ages. Jesus of Nazareth is the centerpiece of God's purposes, and Luke includes ample Old Testament references to prove this. Jesus is not simply another teacher or prophet, and his crucifixion was not a tragic accident. He is the truth that the world hungers for and that God has promised. And his kingdom is the beginning of a new era in human and divine history.

Luke gives special attention to the Holy Spirit as the power behind Jesus's ministry, the power within the church, and the fulfillment of God's promises for humanity. He also emphasizes the radical nature of the new community—the citizens of the kingdom of God. A lot of unexpected people are included in Messiah's kingdom. Luke frequently focuses on the marginalized members of Jewish society—the poor, outcasts, sinners, and even Gentiles and Samaritans. And Luke, more than any other biblical writer, is careful to portray women as vital participants in the community of faith. Unlike the religious structure in Judea in Jesus's day, the kingdom of God is not dominated by highly educated men with relatively high status. It is a broad community in which everyone, even the least likely participant, is treated equally. The point Luke seems to be making is that the gospel is radically different, it defies expectations, and it rankles the existing order. Not only is the kingdom coming, it is clashing with another kingdom. This clash makes the gospel swell with dramatic tension.

A careful reader will notice these themes interwoven throughout the book: The Holy Spirit is mentioned with greater frequency. Women are featured prominently. Outcasts and sinners take center stage remarkably often. Jesus's conflict with the religious establishment grows more intense as the Gospel progresses. And the fulfillment of God's mission is the implied context behind many parables and events. One gets a different flavor of Jesus from reading each of the Gospels as individual pieces. Luke's version is a skilled and well-crafted presentation of the greatest story ever told.

Uniqueness

The Gospel of Luke and the book of Acts are perhaps the only books of the Bible written by a non-Jew. It's possible that Luke was a Greek-speaking Jew; however, his emphasis on the Gentile mission in Acts and his frequent references to Old Testament prophecies that point to God's purposes for Gentiles seem to indicate an unusual personal interest in God's global mission to non-Jews. Most commentators have concluded that Luke was likely a Gentile who was also well acquainted with Jewish history, culture, and faith. If so, his perspective is a unique and significant addition to Scripture.

Nineteen of Luke's thirty-five parables are found only in Luke. Without Luke, we would have no record of Jesus's parables about the prodigal son, the good Samaritan, the rich fool, or persistence in prayer. And Luke includes a lot of historical details not found in the other Gospels too. For example, we would know very little of the Christmas story and Jesus's childhood if not for Luke's Gospel. We would also know nothing of Zacchaeus or how Jesus encountered two disciples on the Emmaus road after his resurrection. It's hard to imagine the story of Jesus without these key parables and events. Luke's contribution to the Gospel records is invaluable.

The Author

Luke was the most skilled writer and the most intentional historian among the Gospel authors. From his opening sentence, it's clear that he saw himself as a reporter of facts. That doesn't mean he was without a strong agenda in writing—Luke clearly presented the evidence of Jesus's ministry for definite theological purposes. But his stated purpose is to give an account and provide clear evidence for faith.

Who was Luke? Paul calls him a doctor (Col. 4:14), and he seems to become an integral part of the picture around the time Paul ministered in Philippi, which had a well-known medical school. Luke may have been from Philippi originally, or he may have lived there because of an affiliation with the school as a graduate or instructor. Many physicians of the time were itinerant companions of influential political, business, or military figures, so it's entirely possible that Luke served in this role for Paul and his companions. It's likely, though not certain, that he's a Gentile rather than a Hellenistic Jew. It's even possible that he's the "Lucius of Cyrene" mentioned in Acts 13:1 and that he simply reconnected with Paul in Philippi, and/or that he's the Lucius mentioned in Romans 16:21. But speculation aside, what we know for certain is that he's an educated man who has both medical and literary skills.

Luke considers himself a historian in the Greek style of compiling a history. He begins his Gospel with a statement of intent: "since I myself have carefully investigated everything from the beginning, it seemed good also to me to write an orderly account for you, most excellent Theophilus, so that you may know the certainty of the things you have been taught" (Luke 1:3–4). His information was "handed down to us by those who from the first were eyewitnesses and servants of the word" (1:2). Luke would certainly have had access to those eyewitnesses and "servants of the word"—those who guarded the stories and early documents on Jesus's ministry. If he was in Jerusalem during the two years that Paul was imprisoned there, as Acts seems to imply, he could have interviewed numerous people who had followed Jesus. He would have spent considerable time in churches that had carefully preserved accurate oral and written testimonies about him. He would likely have seen the reliable evidence compiled by the "many [who had] undertaken to draw up an account of the things that have been fulfilled" (1:1). It's quite possible that Luke and most of Acts were written during this time in Jerusalem.

How to Use This Guide

The discussion guides in this series are intended to create a link between past and present, between the cultural and historical context of the Bible and real life as we experience it today. By putting ourselves as closely into biblical situations as possible, we can begin to understand how God interacted with his people in the past and, therefore, how he interacts with us today. The information in this book makes ancient Scripture relevant to twenty-first-century life as God means for us to live it.

The questions in this book are geared to do what a discussion guide should do: provoke discussion. You won't see obvious "right" answers to most of these questions. That's because biblical characters had to wrestle with deep spiritual issues and didn't have easy, black-and-white answers handed to them. They discovered God's will as he led them and revealed himself to them—the same process we go through today, though we have the added help of their experiences to inform us. Biblical characters experienced God in complex situations, and so do we. By portraying those situations realistically, we learn how to apply the Bible to our own lives. One of the best ways to do that is through in-depth discussion with other believers.

The discussion questions within each session are designed to elicit every participant's input, regardless of his or her level of preparation. Obviously, the more group members prepare by reading the biblical text and the background information in the study guide, the more they will get out of it. But even in busy weeks that afford no preparation time, everyone will be able to participate in a meaningful way.

The discussion questions also allow your group quite a bit of latitude. Some groups prefer to briefly discuss the questions in order to cover as many as possible, while others focus on only one or two of them in order to have more in-depth conversations. Since this study is designed for flexibility, feel free to adapt it according to the personality and needs of your group.

Each session ends with a hypothetical situation that relates to the passage of the week. Discussion questions are provided, but group members may also want to consider role-playing the scenario or setting up a two-team debate over one or two of the questions. These exercises often cultivate insights that wouldn't come out of a typical discussion.

Regardless of how you use this material, the biblical text will always be the ultimate authority. Your discussions may take you to many places and cover many issues, but they will have the greatest impact when they begin and end with God's Word itself. And never forget that the Spirit who inspired the Word is in on the discussion too. May he guide it—and you—wherever he wishes.

Good News of Great Joy

LUKE 1–3

"Victory at all costs, victory in spite of all terror, victory however long and hard the road may be; for without victory, there is no survival." So said Winston Churchill to a meeting of Parliament in the early years of World War II. And he was right—victory would come at an enormous cost. It would require a long and hard road. But it was absolutely necessary.

Great victories cost a lot. Israel's exodus from Egypt was a miraculous victory, but it was also a traumatic event that cost lives and took an entire generation to fully resolve. The American Civil War was brutal, but it won a great victory by keeping a nation united and securing freedom for slaves. On a much smaller but more personal scale, most of us can testify that our greatest accomplishments have generally required years of sacrifice.

There has been no greater victory in human history than the redemption God secured for us by incarnating himself in Jesus. There also has been no greater sacrifice. A tension between the thrill of long-awaited victory and the trauma of painful costs is apparent even in the earliest pages of Luke's Gospel, and it builds all the way to the end when victory and sacrifice meet at the cross. Jesus is presented to us as the fulfillment of ancient hopes and prophecies—a virgin mother, shepherds, angels, and many more erupted in praise—but he came in a humble package that was designed to pay a price. His entrance into this world was not simple or convenient; it was surrounded by controversy and foreshadowed a coming crisis.

You'll probably find that the victories in your life—including your hard-fought accomplishments and the work God is doing in you and through you—are flavored by some of the same dynamics. The Christian life is a cause for great praise, but it isn't easy. It involves both miracles and crises. We may come into God's kingdom through the gloriously free gift of grace, but we can't truly live in the kingdom without experiencing the cost of discipleship. Spiritual growth is accomplished by the power of God, but often through the pain of the soul. It's a trustworthy principle that victory and sacrifice walk hand in hand.

How Will This Be? Luke 1

Focus: Luke 1:26–38

Strange stirrings have already been happening in the family—an old woman conceived a child, and an angel had announced it to her husband as he was carrying out his priestly duties. Now a very young cousin—an unmarried teenager—is visited by the same angel with an even more remarkable message: she will give birth to the Son of the Most High, the Messiah, and name him Yeshua, "the Lord saves."

The sense of responsibility, the sense of privilege, the questions of how and why—it all must have been overwhelming. How could God do something so wonderful, so controversial, so scripturally unprecedented? Why not after she's married, or through someone older or with higher status? The theological reasons and scriptural background for this kind of birth wouldn't be understood until years later, and Mary's reputation wouldn't be fully vindicated until her son grew up and demonstrated who he was. This would be a beautiful, painful, marvelous, heavy responsibility.

Even so, Mary is willing. Her mind can't grasp the significance of the news or how it will be carried out, but her heart accepts Gabriel's words: "nothing is impossible with God" (1:37). May it be so, she answers. Her assignment is staggering, her acceptance of it unwavering.

A SACRED LEGACY

Luke is careful to include echoes of biblical history in his narrative on Elizabeth and Mary. Elizabeth's barrenness fits a common biblical theme: God gave Sarah a child in her old age, waited years to open Rachel's womb, miraculously gave Samson to a previously childless couple, and answered Hannah's desperate prayer to have a child after years of barrenness. Gabriel's words to Mary in Luke 1:38 ("For nothing is impossible with God") are almost identical to God's words regarding Sarah in Genesis 18:14 ("Is anything too hard for the LORD?"). And Mary's song of praise in 1:46–55 is reminiscent of Hannah's song after the birth of Samuel (1 Sam. 2:1–10). These echoes of history announce to the reader that God is once again beginning a great work with miraculous births.

15

Discuss

- What do you think went through Mary's mind when Gabriel delivered his message? What questions would you have had if an angel visited you with such an unexpected message?

  _____

  _____

  _____

  _____

- Why do you think it was important for Jesus to have been born from a virgin?

  _____

  _____

  _____

  _____

A Light for Revelation: Luke 2

Focus: Luke 2:21–40

Jesus is born six months after John, he is circumcised according to the law, and his parents take him to the temple to dedicate Jesus to the Lord and make sacrifices for Mary's purification. They offer a pair of doves or pigeons as allowed for those who are too poor to offer a lamb (Lev. 12:6–8). Mary and Joseph are humble and obedient—an apt representation of the righteous remnant of Israel through whom Messiah is prophesied to come.

While at the temple, unusual signs point to the special nature of this child. A devout man named Simeon, who had been told by the Holy Spirit that he would see the Messiah before his death, is moved by the Spirit to recognize Jesus as the one. He praises God and prophesies over the child. This child, says

Simeon, will be a light to the Gentiles and the glory of Israel. He will be a dividing line, a crisis character, for many—some will be raised up by him, and others will fall. He will be blessed and opposed. And something in his future will pierce his parents' hearts. He will bear great fruit at a great cost.

A prophetess is also at the temple that day. In fact, Anna has been at the temple every day for decades. Widowed at a young age and now eighty-four years old, she has devoted her life to worship, prayer, and fasting. She, too, recognizes the Messiah and thanks God for having seen him. The spirit of prophecy, long latent in Israel's history, is being rekindled by the presence of the Son of God.

Discuss

- How do you think Simeon and Anna were able to recognize a baby as the Messiah? How had they become so in tune with the Holy Spirit?

  _____

  _____

  _____

  _____

- Psalm 126:5 says that those who sow in tears will reap with joy—a dynamic Simeon points to by prophesying both the blessing and the pain of parenting Jesus. Have you found this principle to be true in your life—that the greater the fruit you bear, the greater the cost in bearing it? If so, how?

  _____

  _____

  _____

  _____

THEY ASKED

Zechariah responded to Gabriel's announcement of John's conception with a question: "How can I be sure of this?" (Luke 1:18). Mary also responded to his announcement of Jesus's conception with a question: "How will this be?" (Luke 1:34). Zechariah was rebuked for doubting, while Mary was given an explanation. What was the difference? Apparently Zechariah's question came from doubt—he wasn't sure it could happen. Mary's question seems to have come from amazement at how such a marvelous thing could be accomplished—she knew it could happen but didn't know how. The difference in wording is subtle but profound. God rebukes questions that come from unbelief but honors those that seek to understand his ways.

The Voice and the Son: Luke 3

Focus: Luke 3:15–22

"Jochanon the Immerser" comes preaching the "good news" as a voice in the wilderness. It is harsh news to some—to those at odds with the coming kingdom—and John is quite confrontational about it. He has rebuked the puppet king of Judea, warned the religious leaders of the wrath coming against them, and urged powerful tax collectors and soldiers to clean up their act. This forerunner is Messiah-like, but he isn't the Messiah. He prophesies of the true King, who will offer a baptism of Spirit and fire.

One day the Messiah comes to be baptized in the river. This act is a mystery to many; he is not repenting or being cleansed of his sin, because he has no sin nor need for repentance. He is the standard to which all others must conform. Why, then, is he baptized? Is his baptism on behalf of his people? Is he identifying as a Son of Man with those who will need him? Is he simply modeling the right actions? Regardless of the reason, this is a landmark day in his ministry. He is commissioned for the work ahead, fully identified as the Son of God by a voice from heaven and a physical manifestation of the Spirit upon him. In a mind-stretching paradox, this invisible Spirit comes "in bodily form"—like a dove, we are told. And the voice from heaven declares the identity of the Son, the Father's love for him, and the divine pleasure in their relationship.

Discuss

- What do you think John meant by baptism with the Holy Spirit and with fire? Do you think most Christians can relate to this? Why or why not?

_____

_____

_____

_____

A CASE STUDY

Imagine: An angel appears to you with a startling announcement: The Lord wants to do an amazing work through you that will change the world forever. His plan will cost you your dreams for the future and cause many people to look at you suspiciously for the rest of your life. It will make you one of heaven's heroes of faith but rip your heart apart in the process. The Lord will not force you to accept this assignment; you have complete freedom to choose, and he will love and accept you regardless. If you decline, you will still live a fruitful, uneventful, but generally satisfying life. If you accept, you will experience radical fulfillment beyond your dreams along with excruciating pain that you wouldn't wish on anyone.

- In all honesty, would you choose to accept this assignment? Would you rather have a moderately satisfying life with no real highs or lows or experience the extremes of both pleasure and pain?
- How many details would you need to know before being able to say, "I am the Lord's servant . . . may it be to me as you have said"?
- "The greater the work of God, the greater the trauma involved in it." Does that statement inspire you to seek greatness in God's kingdom or to shy away from it? Why?

Beyond Expectations

LUKE 4–6

The Protestant Reformation, the Moravian movement, the American Great Awakenings, the Wesleyan movement, and the Welsh revival of the early 1900s are generally accepted among evangelicals today as movements inspired by the Holy Spirit. We have seen the fruit and, while acknowledging the flaws and imperfections of those involved, recognize that God was at work. Yet all were criticized harshly in their time. Plenty of honest, Bible-believing people argued that these movements were not from God. They were controversial, their leaders often interpreted biblical truth in a way that stretched the prevailing understanding of the day, and they inspired unfamiliar practices. Some critics even called these movements satanic.

So why do we recognize today that God was at work in them? Because we've seen the end of the story. These newfangled trends became accepted practices and developed solid institutions. What once seemed abnormal became normal. Once the controversy dissipated, we were able to see the Spirit.

But what if we, as modern observers, stepped into these movements as they were beginning? Would we recognize God at work? Or what if, to take it back even further, we stepped into Jesus's ministry in the middle of the story? Would we be able to see the Spirit's movements on the spot? Would we be able to put aside our expectations and our long-held paradigms and think outside the spiritual box?

Many people of Jesus's day couldn't set their expectations and paradigms aside. They didn't have a grid for understanding what God was doing. Some could, however. They were usually the ones whose expectations and paradigms had been shattered long before—the misfits, the outcasts, the violators of the status quo. Those who were simply hungry for God were able to see him at work. Those who were entrenched in the religious culture were just as entrenched in their narrow thinking.

There were exceptions, of course. Luke makes it clear that Jesus received a variety of responses. Most Pharisees were annoyed by him, but some saw God in him. Most of the common people were intrigued by him, but some were *only* intrigued while others were thoroughly captivated by his love and power. The testimony of Luke's Gospel is that while the true identity of Jesus was recognizable, it often went unrecognized. Like virtually all true works of the Holy Spirit, Jesus's ministry encountered resistance and sparked controversy.

It's interesting to speculate about whether we would have recognized Jesus for who he was if we lived when he was on earth, but that's only a hypothetical question. The real issue is whether we recognize God at work now. If we marvel at how he shattered expectations in the first century but think he would fit conveniently into ours now, we're fooling ourselves. We can discern the true work of God only when we're hungry for him—as he truly is, regardless of the "package" he comes in. In order to see him, we have to have willing hearts, be sensitive to who he is and how he works, and ask him to open our eyes.

Hometown "Hero": Luke 4

Focus: Luke 4:16–30

Fresh off of his baptism, at which all three members of the Trinity had been tangibly present, Jesus is full of the Spirit and driven by the Spirit to be tempted in the wilderness. The adversary urges him to abuse divine privileges and offers him exactly what he wants—the kingdoms of the world. But Jesus defers his desire for the nations in order to win them in the right way at the right time through the people who love him. He resists every temptation and returns in the power of the Spirit to Galilee, where he speaks in many Galilean synagogues.

One of those synagogues is in his hometown of Nazareth, and for a brief moment in time, Jesus is the city's favorite son. He reads the Torah scroll, a messianic portion from Isaiah 61, and then declares that this Scripture has been fulfilled by none other than himself. Some in the audience marvel that "Joseph's son" would say such a thing, but his words are gracious and well received—until he emphasizes that his ministry will not be accepted in his hometown and that he will minister among Gentiles as Elijah and Elisha did. This less-than-favorable indictment of hometown provincialism and Jewish exclusivity infuriates the crowd, and the favorite son immediately becomes a goat. They try to throw Jesus off the edge of a cliff, but he somehow passes through the crowd and escapes.

Jesus continues his ministry in Galilee—the city of Capernaum, more specifically—for a time. He delivers a demoniac and heals Peter's mother-in-law. But by the end of chapter 4 he has moved on from Galilee and is ministering in the synagogues of Judea.

Discuss

- Why do you think the crowd was surprised by Jesus's words and the comparison of his ministry to that of Elijah and Elisha? In what ways does the ministry of Jesus defy your

JESUS AT THE SYNAGOGUE

Luke says it was Jesus's custom to go to synagogue on the Sabbath, and his reputation as a teacher was strong enough that he was asked to read the Torah scroll at Nazareth's synagogue. It's unclear whether he read Isaiah 61:1–2 by choice or according to the lectionary schedule. Regardless, the messianic text is ideal for introducing Jesus. Interestingly, he takes the liberty to omit one line from the original prophecy (about binding up the brokenhearted from Isaiah 61:1); adds a line from Isaiah 58:6 (about setting the oppressed free); and cuts off the reading mid-sentence, immediately before "the day of vengeance of our God" (Isa. 61:2), a role that fits his second coming rather than his first. This kind of oral editing was acceptable for respected teachers, though more so when reading the prophets than when reading the law of Moses. With this careful compilation of verses, Jesus boldly declared that he was the Messiah, the fulfillment of prophecy.

expectations of what a Messiah should be and do in your life?

_____

_____

_____

_____

Unconventional: Luke 5

Focus: Luke 5:12–31

After calling some fishermen to follow him, Jesus demonstrates his authority to cleanse lepers, to heal diseases, and even to forgive sins. The power over disease and impurity should have been enough to validate his authority—the religious leaders should recognize that miracles of healing come from God. But when Jesus sees the efforts of four men trying to help their paralyzed friend, he responds to their faith by forgiving the paralytic. This, of course, is blasphemy to a Jewish mind steeped in Scripture. Only God can forgive the sins of the heart because all sins are ultimately against him. So the teachers of the law, assuming that this miracle worker from Nazareth could not possibly be God, regardless of whether he's the Messiah, condemn him for doing what only God can do. His words and actions don't fit the grid of their understanding. So Jesus tells the paralytic to get up and walk as evidence of his divine authority to undo the effects of sin and brokenness.

An even further stretch for the religious leaders is Jesus's willingness to socialize with reviled extortionists—the tax collectors of the day. He willingly attends a banquet given by one of these government-sanctioned thieves, a man named Levi who, for the sake of profit, has clearly cast his lot with Israel's enemies, the Romans. Nevertheless, Jesus eats and drinks with

Levi, and the Pharisees are incensed. Their outrage prompts a landmark statement in Jesus's ministry: "It is not the healthy who need a doctor, but the sick. I have not come to call the righteous, but sinners to repentance" (5:31).

As the chapter closes, Jesus sums up the conflict. The religious authorities have an old wineskin of understanding, but Jesus brings new wine. Old wineskins break when filled with new wine. Therefore, a new wineskin is needed. Only a new understanding—a new perspective, a new paradigm—can handle the radical, expectation-defying ministry of the Messiah.

Discuss

- Do you think our churches are known more as places for the righteous to gather or as hospitals where the sick can get better? How well does Christianity today line up with Jesus's mission statement in 5:31?

_____

_____

_____

_____

Choosing a Foundation: Luke 6

Focus: Luke 6:17–26, 46–49

Jesus's violations of the Jewish leadership's expectations continue—he heals on the Sabbath, for example—and they are furious. By this time, their anger goes beyond words, and they begin to discuss "what they might do" to him (6:11).

Jesus addresses a large crowd of disciples who have gathered around him for healing and deliverance. His message—many of the same truths he preached in the Sermon on the Mount as it is presented in Matthew—includes the characteristics of those who are blessed and those who experience woe; the radical nature of God's kind of love and mercy; how human beings are meant to embrace that kind of love and mercy; what it means to bear good fruit; and the wisdom of building a life based on Jesus's words. And with one pointed question, Jesus sums up the discrepancy between superficial and real faith: "Why do you call me 'Lord, Lord,' and do not do what I say?" (6:46).

Discuss

- In what areas have you seen other Christians call Jesus Lord but not do what he says? In what ways have you done this?

_____

_____

_____

_____

SPIRIT OF POWER

Luke writes in 6:19 that "power was coming from him." Treating spiritual power as a tangible reality is a common theme in this Gospel: the power of the Most High overshadowed Mary (1:35); Jesus returned to Galilee in the power of the Spirit (4:14); the people were amazed at the power coming from Jesus (4:36); the power of the Lord was present for him to heal (5:17); he noticed the power going from him toward a woman who touched his clothes in secret (8:46); he imparted power to the twelve disciples (9:1) and to the seventy-two disciples (10:19); and he promised to clothe his followers with "power from on high" (24:49).

27

A Case Study

Imagine: The "rising star" on the religious landscape is considered one of today's most effective communicators, and his popularity exploded almost overnight. Much of the negative attention he has received is due to his extravagant claims about himself, his blatantly offensive comments about current religious leadership, his unconventional spin on well-known Bible verses, and his sharp opposition to many church traditions. But he has also done quite a few miracles (at least that's what his devotees claim), he does have some fascinating and profound ideas, and he seems genuinely compassionate toward normal, everyday people. You've asked your spiritual mentors what they think of him, and they mostly disapprove. Their reasons? Controversy and conflict follow him everywhere, he's too caustic with those who disagree with him, and his teachings are "a lot of truth mixed with just enough error to be dangerous." But while you can certainly see some unusual angles in his teaching, you can't put your finger on the errors. Still, conventional wisdom says this eccentric crowd-pleaser is a passing novelty and a potential fraud.

- How would you respond to a religious teacher like this? What would he have to do to prove to you that he was from God?

- In what ways does the above description fit Jesus—or at least the way he was perceived by religious leaders in Israel?

- Do you think most Christians today would have accepted Jesus in his time, before having read the end of the story? If you met Jesus in the middle of the Gospels—before the cross and resurrection—do you think you would have accepted him? Why or why not?

Clash of Kingdoms

LUKE 7–8

Two kingdoms can't occupy the same territory—not without fierce conflict eventually erupting. Kingdoms are predicated on the idea of exercising sovereignty, and sovereignty is an exclusive right. No one person or place can have two "highest" authorities. When two parties vie for control, battles break out.

Much of Luke is a picture of kingdoms clashing. As Jesus's kingdom of light breaks into the darkness of the world, the illegitimate ruler of the world's systems—the captor of human souls—fights back. In the upcoming chapters we see conflict between Jesus and demons, the Spirit and religiosity, life and death. We see the kingdom of God redefining relationships, basing the idea of family on faith rather than genetics. The

29

incoming King demonstrates his authority over disease, death, sin, weather patterns, and demons.

The religious experts don't like it. Jesus compares them to children in the marketplace who play a tune and expect others to dance accordingly. But Jesus dances to a different beat. He hears God's voice and refuses to allow lesser voices to dictate his life. And, as we will see, he expects his followers to do the same.

That's why it's important to ask ourselves which tune we're dancing to. Are we in sync with the rhythms of God? Or are we falling in step with whatever the world is playing? Are we directed by God's voice or driven by the demands of other people? The call to follow Jesus is a call to stop following lesser rulers. In the midst of a clash of kingdoms, it's important to know the difference.

Awkward Encounter: Luke 7

Focus: Luke 7:36–50

It was common for religious intelligentsia to invite traveling teachers to a meal in order to further discuss spiritual matters.

ECHOES OF THE PAST

About nine centuries before Jesus, Elisha prayed for the dead son of a woman from Shunem, and the young man was raised back to life (2 Kings 4:8–37). When Jesus approached Nain, he encountered a widow coming out of the city in a funeral procession for her son—her only means of support—and his heart went out to her (Luke 7:11–17). He touched the coffin and the dead man sat up and began to talk. Not only was this a profound event in its own right; it also connected Jesus with Elisha. Nain was on the opposite side of the hill from Shunem—the site of the ancient prophet's most famous miracle.

30

Apparently Simon the Pharisee has heard Jesus speak and extended such an invitation. Simon's like-minded friends would have all been welcomed, and villagers would have been allowed to wander in and stand at a distance from the tables to observe the meal and listen to the discussion.

But it's clear that Simon does not respect Jesus as an equal. He does not arrange for Jesus's feet to be washed, nor does he greet Jesus with a formal kiss. It's the Middle Eastern equivalent of a Western dinner party in which the host opens the door, casually turns his back to the guest of honor, doesn't offer to take the guest's coat or introduce him to other attendees, and mutters "Oh, you came." Jesus makes no remark about this inhospitable reception—not yet, anyway. To do so would have been an equal breach of etiquette, and Jesus doesn't lower himself to that. He knows he is there to be scrutinized and likely rebutted by "discerning" spiritual leaders for all he has said to the crowds. He does nothing to heighten the tension.

Someone else does, however. A woman with a shady reputation has come, and she notices the rude reception Jesus receives. She boldly moves to the table where Jesus is reclining and wets his feet with her tears. She lets down her hair—a very personal gesture a respectable peasant woman would make only in the presence of her husband—and uses it to wipe his feet. Then she puts her lips to this basest, most offensive part of the human body, and pours perfume over them. Simon, who has likely invited Jesus in order to prove through conversation that this teacher is no prophet, already has his answer. If the teacher had any divine discernment at all, he would know this woman's sordid reputation throughout the town.

"I have something to say to you," Jesus says to Simon, reading the Pharisee's thoughts. The idiomatic statement is a blunt warning that a direct confrontation is coming. Jesus is bold to respond—in Middle Eastern hospitality it's practically unheard of for a guest to rebuke a host. But Simon's complete inability to recognize a sinner's repentance and God's forgiving grace cannot go unchallenged. Jesus presents the Pharisee with a simple parable about two debtors who had no means to pay their debts. One was forgiven of a huge sum, the other of a more modest amount. Which one would be more grateful? The one whose debt was greater. In this brief exchange, Jesus has made two profound and powerful statements: (1) God's great grace is available to all who receive it, and (2) Jesus himself is the unique mediator who offers it.

Discuss

- In what ways, if any, do you think the kind of judgmentalism demonstrated by Simon is reflected in Christians and churches today? What can we do to cultivate more of a culture of grace?

  _____

  _____

  _____

  _____

The Word of Life: Luke 8

Focus: Luke 8:4–15

Jesus compares his preaching—and the Word of God in general—to seed sown by a farmer. In Palestine a farmer would carry a bag of seed as he walked through paths in his field, tossing and scattering the seed into the plowed ground. Some would fall on the path itself and yield no fruit. Other seed would fall

JESUS AND WOMEN

More than any other Gospel writer, Luke emphasizes the role of women in Jesus's ministry and teaching. Chapter 7 ends with a highly unusual interaction with a woman at a banquet, and chapter 8 begins with a revolutionary portrait of women following Jesus. Mary Magdalene, Joanna (the wife of a prominent political figure), Susanna, "and many others" (8:3) were all traveling with him and supporting him financially. Luke often records Jesus's parables in doublets with a male-centered and female-centered focus. For example, the kingdom of God is like a mustard seed sown by a man and like leaven hidden by a woman (13:18–21). A shepherd goes after his lost sheep, and a woman seeks a lost coin (15:1–10). The men of Nineveh and the queen of Sheba will both be honored above Jesus's listeners in the judgment (11:29–32). Jesus tells two parables about persistence in prayer, one involving a male neighbor (11:5–8) and the other involving a widow (18:1–8). Commentators generally agree that Luke is intentionally making a point: the kingdom of God is radically countercultural in the role it affords women.

on shallow soil over rocks and, after initially sprouting, would succumb to the dryness of its root system. Some seed would fall among thorns and weeds and lose out in the fierce competition for the soil's nutrients. Most of the seed, one would hope, would fall into rich, well-plowed soil, where it would grow and yield a great harvest. So it is with those who hear the message of the kingdom.

The disciples ask for an explanation of the parable. Apparently they also ask why Jesus uses so many parables in the first place. The kingdom is full of secrets and mysteries, he says, drawing on a common biblical theme (see Dan. 2:20–23 and 29–30, for example). Parables accomplish two purposes: they reveal secrets to those whose hearts can accept them, and they

33

hide secrets from those whose hearts would be further hardened by them. Those who hear divine mysteries have a choice either to pursue understanding or to turn away from the mysteries altogether, thereby revealing the level of their hunger for truth and for God. Jesus shares his truth with those who are ready to hear and believe it—those who will water it, cultivate it, and bear much fruit by doing so.

Discuss

- What possible reasons can you think of for Jesus revealing truth in a way that only some can understand it?

  _____

  _____

  _____

  _____

- What kind of "hearer" have you been at various stages in your life? What kind of hearers have you observed in the people around you?

  _____

  _____

  _____

  _____

Focus: 8:40–56

Jesus and his disciples had sailed across the lake from Galilee. After a dramatic scene in which Jesus casts a multitude of demons out of a raging lunatic and into a herd of pigs, the men return to the Galilean side. They are greeted by a crowd and by a synagogue ruler named Jairus, who falls at Jesus's feet and begs him to help his dying daughter. The situation is urgent.

A woman who has been hemorrhaging for twelve years is among the crowd. Her flow of blood has made her constantly ritually unclean, prohibiting her from visiting the temple and fully participating in Israel's worship. She isn't treated as a sinner—everyone is ritually unclean from time to time—but the degree and length of her uncleanness has effectually rendered her a religious and perhaps social outcast. She knows Jesus can heal her, but she has to touch him in secret—from behind. She aims to slip through the crowd and back out of it unnoticed.

She manages to touch the fringes of Jesus's garment—perhaps the tassels called *tzitzit* that hang from the four corners of his prayer shawl. After all, this is the sun of righteousness who has healing in his "wings" (Mal. 4:2)—another name for the *tzitzit*. But her plan of remaining hidden is foiled when Jesus notices that power has gone out from him and says so rather loudly. The entire crowd stops along with him, and the spotlight falls on her. Her healing has turned into one of her most embarrassing moments—but only briefly. As she tremblingly confesses her covert healing, Jesus affirms her faith and blesses her to go in peace.

Meanwhile, a very impatient father with a dying daughter stands waiting. And, as it turns out, Jesus has taken too long. A messenger reports that the daughter is dead. But Jesus presses on. "Don't be afraid," he tells the synagogue leader. "Just believe." Jesus arrives at the house, passes through the crowd of wailing mourners, and endures the mocking of those who assure him the girl is already dead. He then takes three disciples and the parents into the room with him and tells the girl to wake up. When she sits up, Jesus urges her parents to feed her. It's an astonishing turn of events. Jesus has once again overcome death and shown himself to be a master over desperate situations.

Discuss

- Needy and desperate, the hemorrhaging woman overcame fear, risked embarrassment, and pushed her way through a thick crowd to get to Jesus. Do you think her attitudes and actions are an appropriate model for our prayers? Why or why not? How do you think Jesus normally responds to need, desperation, risky faith, and persistence?

_____

_____

A CASE STUDY

Imagine: You were desperate for God to help, and you prayed your heart out. But God's timing was much slower than yours, and eventually your hope began to fade. Your prayers weakened and the crisis passed—unresolved, unaddressed, and seemingly unredeemed. God may have heard your prayers, but he was too slow in answering them. His silence—or was it a "no" answer?—remains a mystery to you. And deep down inside, you wonder whether you can trust him in your times of greatest need.

- In what ways can you relate to this scenario? In what situations has God remained silent far longer than you wanted him to?

- What happens to our faith and hope when God delays his answers to our crises? Do situations like this tend to strengthen our faith or undermine our trust? Why?

- If you've ever experienced a situation in which Jesus seemed to be taking too long, in what ways does the story of Jairus's daughter encourage you? In God's kingdom, is it ever too late to hope? Why or why not?

God on a Mission

LUKE 9–11

God is active. A lot of people don't know that. Some philo-sophical systems portray him as static, not only unmovable but unmoving, always there but seldom actually doing anything. Some see him as simply a presence or a state of being—the impersonal cause that no longer causes very much.

But the first image of God in Scripture is of an active Creator, and the first image of the Holy Spirit shows him hovering, mov-ing back and forth across the surface of the waters, breathing his breath into creation and causing life and order to spring up. He is portrayed throughout the Bible as a personal being who relates to us with interpersonal dynamics. He has desires and plans and feelings and thoughts and zeal. He is a God on a relentless mission.

There's a lot of movement in this section of Luke. The Spirit who moved over the surface of the deep waters in Genesis is moving and breathing over the landscape of the earth to instill life into his people. Jesus sends out twelve disciples, and they return; then he sends out seventy-two disciples, and they return. These chapters tell us that he sent messengers into Samaria, that he "resolutely set out for Jerusalem" (9:51), and that he even discussed the coming "exodus" with some ancient men of faith who knew quite a bit about the movements of God.

Luke 9:51 begins a long section (through chapter 19) designated by many as "the travel narrative." The city of Jerusalem figures prominently in this portion of Luke—the section begins and ends with Jerusalem, Jesus sets his face toward Jerusalem, and he laments over Jerusalem twice. And the movements of the Messiah and his disciples virtually cover the landscape between his northern ministry in Galilee and his destination at a cross on a hill in the holy city. He is an accurate picture of the biblical Father—a God on a mission.

It's clear that Jesus expected his disciples to be on that same mission. He sent them out on multiple occasions in order to preach the good news and do miracles in his name. He gave them authority over the power of the enemy, and they used it. They came back with good reports of demons bowing to the pressure of their words. And those who hunger for God hear his Word being preached.

There's no reason that Christians today shouldn't take up that same mission. In fact, we're commanded to. We may not have been present the day Jesus granted his followers authority over snakes and scorpions and all the power of the enemy, but other verses imply that this authority extends throughout the ages to all who believe. Like the Spirit and the Son, we can move over the face of the earth in his authority to breathe his life into his fallen creation. We, too, were designed to be an accurate picture of the biblical Father—a God on a mission.

Revelation of Authority: Luke 9

Focus: Luke 9:18–36

Jesus sends the twelve disciples out on a village-to-village mission, giving them power and authority over demons and diseases. When they return, they withdraw to a town called Bethsaida. But this debriefing is not the retreat it was meant to be—the crowds follow. When the time comes to disperse the crowds into surrounding villages for food, Jesus urges his disciples to feed them instead. Miraculously, the Lord turns a few fishes and loaves into enough food for five thousand men plus the women and children who had come.

Jesus's ministry is at its height of popularity. "Who do the crowds say I am?" he asks his disciples one day. They give a range of responses, but Peter nails the correct answer by affirming that Jesus is the long-awaited Messiah. Jesus warns that he won't fit the people's messianic expectations. This Messiah—and all who follow him—must live a life of sacrifice.

About a week later, Jesus takes Peter, James, and John up a mountain to pray. Jesus's appearance changes, Moses and Elijah appear, and Jesus discusses with them the "departure"—literally, the "exodus"—that he is about to fulfill. The disciples emerge from their sleepiness and see the glory around them, and as Moses and Elijah are leaving, a thick cloud envelops the mountaintop. A voice from the cloud evokes a long-ago prophecy from Deuteronomy 18:15–19 about the Prophet who would one day come. "Listen to him," say both the ancient prophecy and the present voice. And when the cloud lifts, only Jesus remains. The disciples tell no one what they've seen.

Discuss

- Throughout Luke's Gospel, and repeatedly in chapter 9, Jesus demonstrates both power and authority. But these related concepts aren't identical. What does it look like for a person to accept his authority? What does it look like for a person to experience his power? What's the difference between the two? In what ways are they related?

_____

_____

_____

_____

Exercise of Power: Luke 10

Focus: Luke 10:21–37

Again, Jesus sends out his disciples—this time seventy-two of them. He gives them authority over all the power of the enemy and to trample on the enemy's works. When those who were sent out return with good reports, Jesus rejoices and makes a major statement about his ministry and the way God has chosen to work: "I praise you, Father, Lord of heaven and earth, because you have hidden these things from the wise and learned, and revealed them to little children" (10:21). The Father and Son have a unique relationship, and the only people who can know the Father are those to whom the Son has chosen to reveal him. Many prophets and kings have sought this knowledge; only those who have come to Jesus in faith have received it.

A legal expert inquires of Jesus for two reasons: "to test Jesus" (10:25) and "to justify himself" (10:29). An ancient law from Leviticus orders love for one's neighbor, but religious scholars have long debated exactly who a *neighbor* is. All believe the term to include Jews; some believe it to include proselytes to Judaism; and practically none believe it to include Gentiles. So the expert asks: "Who is my neighbor?" In response, Jesus tells a story.

A traveler from Jerusalem to Jericho was robbed, beaten, and left helpless by the side of the road. A priest passed by and had ample opportunity to help but perhaps more reason not to: fear of robbers still in the area, the chance of being ritually defiled by approaching a dead body, the possibility that the wounded or dead man was a non-Jew and therefore not a neighbor, and more. The law to love a neighbor was conditional on the definition of *neighbor*, but the law to remain undefiled was unconditional. The safe thing for a priest to do, in order to obey God's law, was to pass by. Soon, a Levite came upon the victim. He was not bound by the same restrictions, but he faced the same fear of robbers and the added potential of implicitly

JESUS AS THE SAMARITAN

The parable of the Good Samaritan has long been understood simply as a call to compassion, but many commentators throughout church history have seen more to the story than that. Jesus was considered by many to be an outsider—his opponents even went so far in John 8:48 as to call him a Samaritan—and an unlikely candidate to be the Messiah. Yet at great sacrifice, he rescues those who, spiritually speaking, have been beaten and stripped by the enemy and left for dead, and who have no means to repay their rescuer. It is entirely possible that Jesus meant for his hearers to understand not only that they should "go and do likewise," but also that he is like the unexpected Samaritan who binds up wounds and demonstrates God's compassion for those who are helpless.

criticizing the priest who had just traveled that section of the road. To stop and help could be seen as an affront to the priest's interpretation of the law.

Next, Jesus says, a Samaritan passed by—the least likely candidate to show up in a spiritual parable. The bitterness between Jews and Samaritans ran deep. Not many years before, Samaritans had defiled the Jewish temple by scattering bones in the temple court during Passover. They were publicly cursed in synagogues. To make a Samaritan the hero of a story could incite a riot. Yet Jesus tells how this Samaritan risked his own life by stopping where thieves have recently been at work and carrying a half-dead Jew to a local inn. In other words, he showed up in public with enough evidence for Samaritan-hating residents to lynch him on the spot for the crime of beating up a Jew. He bound up the victim's wounds and amply paid the innkeeper for all expenses. Without regard to time, effort, and expense—precise definitions of the requirements of the law—the Samaritan had sacrificial compassion. This, says Jesus, is what it means to be a neighbor.

Discuss

- In what ways do you think Christians today, like the priest and Levite, justify not helping people in need?

_____

_____

_____

Persistence: Luke 11

Focus: Luke 11:1–13

The disciples ask for a lesson in prayer, and Jesus gives them an example of how to pray. Then he tells a parable about boldness and persistence. A man received a visitor at midnight but had no food to set before them. Cultural rules for hospitality demand a meal for hungry travelers, and because the hospitality of one person reflects the hospitality of the entire village, there's a certain expectation for community support. So the host tries to wake a friend and ask for bread. But the friend is sleepy and reluctant. He balks. The man persists. And because of his persistence, his request is eventually granted.

That's a picture of prayer, Jesus says. God isn't a sleepy neighbor, but he does invite bold and persistent requests. Keep asking, keep seeking, keep knocking, Jesus tells his followers. And fully expect that God will give the Holy Spirit to any who ask in this way.

Discuss

- How long do you generally pray for something before you decide to give up? How can we know when to persist in prayer and when God's silence means "no"?

_____

_____

_____

_____

A Case Study

Imagine: You're walking down a city sidewalk at night, and as you pass by a dark alley, you hear a groan. You stop and look into the alley, trying to let your eyes adjust, and can barely make out the shape of a person lying on the ground. Your mind races with the possibilities: a drunk who passed out, a homeless guy try-

PROTECTED

Jesus made a sweeping promise to the seventy-two disciples: "I have given you authority to trample on snakes and scorpions and to overcome all the power of the enemy; nothing will harm you" (10:19). Though this verse doesn't promise us a trouble-free life, it does encourage us to trust God's protection over us at all times. The images seem to be drawn from a psalm of protection: "You will tread upon the lion and the cobra; you will trample the great lion and the serpent" (Ps. 91:13)—the same psalm Satan quoted when trying to tempt Jesus in 4:10–11. Here, Jesus turns the promise back against the enemy.

ing to get some sleep, someone pretending to be injured to lure unsuspecting passersby into the alley to rob them—or someone who is actually hurt and needs help. If you had your cell phone with you, you'd just call 911 and be on your way, but you don't. You have to make a decision whether or not to help.

- In all honesty, what do you think you would do? Which emotion would be stronger: compassion for a potentially hurt stranger, fear of what might happen to you if you help, or confidence that whoever is lying there is probably used to it?

- Do you generally stop and help people in trouble, or do you assume that someone else will help them? How much time and expense do you think you would be willing to sacrifice to help someone who is slightly injured? What about someone with life-threatening injuries?

- To what degree do you think you can expect God to protect you and provide for you when you go out on a limb to help someone?

Culture Conflict

LUKE 12–14

José Bové was annoyed and he wasn't going to take it anymore. So in 1999, the activist farmer drove his tractor through a McDonald's that was being constructed in Millau, France. It was a statement against globalization, against the use of non-local farm products, against the Americanization of French society. It was a counterattack in a culture war.

The term *culture war* has been used to describe the tensions and resentments between civilizations vying for the same people, a conflict between groups holding different social/political/ religious values, and the friction between conservative and progressive movements within a society. The more deeply held the cultural values are, the more violent the war is. That's because people don't compromise their core values easily. A cultural identity is worth fighting for.

Luke 11 ended with a hostile confrontation between Jesus and his opponents—and an ominous statement about their plans against him. The clash of kingdoms was coming to the surface. But in chapter 12, Jesus explains *why* the kingdom of God conflicts so much with the kingdoms of this world. The kingdoms do not share the same values. The world honors wealth, while the kingdom honors simplicity and trust. The world's way of pursuing comfort and security really produces fear and anxiety, while having the right priorities allows us to rest and experience God's provision. Gentleness and humility get people further in God's kingdom than pride and selfishness do. As Jesus pointed out in chapter 6—his sermon on beatitudes, woes, love, mercy—the attitudes and actions of a disciple run contrary to the culture of a fallen world.

Those of us who follow Jesus need to be aware of the culture war going on inside our own hearts. We're caught between two kingdoms vying for our attention. Will we embrace the values of God's kingdom or pursue the things of the world? It's possible to proclaim faith in Jesus without rearranging our priorities to fit his kingdom, but we miss out on experiencing his peace and security when we do. Those who seek "things" may get them, but not with the security those things were thought to provide. Those who seek the kingdom, however, get the kingdom plus the things they need.

The culture war between Jesus's message and the world's ways continues throughout Luke. Sometimes it will surface as a religious conflict between the Messiah and the established authorities, sometimes it will show up as a sinner repenting (i.e., rejecting one set of values for another), and sometimes it will appear as a call to look beyond circumstances and into eternity.

Every time, the reader is confronted with a choice of which kingdom to embrace. Jesus will make it clear that while his kingdom involves sacrifice, the alternatives involve permanent loss. Only one way leads to life. The ultimate winner of the war between kingdoms has already been decided.

Don't Worry: Luke 12

Focus: Luke 12:13–34

Like any regular speaker—itinerant preachers or campaigning politicians, for example—Jesus delivers the same message in multiple venues. One of those messages, recorded as the Sermon on the Mount in Matthew 5–7, is divided in Luke between chapters 6 and 12. In chapter 12, Jesus repeats his well-known teaching on the pointlessness of worry, again drawing attention to how God cares for the flowers of the field and the birds of the air. "Do not worry about your life, what you will eat; or about your body, what you will wear . . . but seek his kingdom, and these things will be given to you as well" (12:22, 31). This lesson comes in response to a listener's request for Jesus to render judgment in an inheritance dispute. Jesus will have no part in it. Instead, he points to the man's preoccupation with his possessions and his rights as a sign of misplaced priorities. Jesus tells a parable about a rich man who sought comfort and wealth without regard to his eternal condition. He follows it with a very strong warning: "Watch out! Be on your guard against all kinds of greed" (12:15).

Discuss

- Many parables and statements in Luke portray those who seek wealth in a negative light. What do you think Jesus

47

would say to the Western church if he were preaching about wealth and materialism today?

_____

_____

_____

Focus: Luke 12:49–56

Jesus has just warned his hearers to be ready for him, both now and in his eventual return. It's further evidence for Luke's theme of fulfillment—that Jesus is the culmination of Scripture's prophecies, the inauguration of a new age of the kingdom. Now this Prince of Peace declares that he has come not to bring peace but to cause division. He is a lightning rod of controversy. In fact, he is bringing fire on the earth and is zealous to see it kindled. And with a clear statement drawn from Micah 7:6 that he will be a sharp dividing line among human beings, even within families, he prophesies his own suffering and warns his hearers that they are not recognizing the signs of the times. The divine nature of his message ought to be as obvious as weather patterns coming off the Mediterranean. The Messiah has come, but those who are not prepared for the trauma of his message and his upcoming ministry will not discern who he is.

Discuss

- How have you seen Jesus cause division among people? How does Jesus's message about his own divisiveness conflict with today's cultural values?

_____

_____

_____

CUSTOMS OF THE FEAST

Kenneth Bailey, a New Testament scholar who has lived most of his life in the Middle East, offers fascinating insight into the social customs surrounding the parable of the banquet. According to traditional customs, guests receive an initial invitation to a feast and, if they accept, are bound to follow through and attend because of the expense to the host in killing an animal and preparing the right amount of food. When the feast has been prepared, a second invitation is extended to let guests know the time has come. This is where Jesus's parable begins—with the second invitation to guests who have already committed to attend. But the guests in the parable offer ridiculous excuses. The first says he is going to examine a field he has already bought—despite the fact that fields in the agrarian Middle East have always been purchased only after every inch of the property and its extensive history have been examined. The same dynamic applies to purchasing oxen—the second guest's excuse. And the third excuse is just as transparent; a wedding could not have just taken place in the village because the host would not have scheduled his banquet to coincide with weeklong marriage festivities, which were known far in advance. These guests assume their rejection of the host will humiliate him. Undeterred, the host finds other guests of lower social status and, according to custom, "compels" them to come in. Why? Because etiquette demands that those of lower social status decline an initial invitation until the host has insisted several times that the invitation is sincere. All of these elements in Jesus's parable accentuate the dramatic confrontation between Jesus and his opponents.

Come and Eat: Luke 14

Focus: Luke 14:16–33

In chapter 13, Jesus has clashed with religious authorities, told some pointed parables implying that many of them will not enter the kingdom, and lamented over Jerusalem. Now he continues the theme with another parable of the kingdom. He pulls an image of God's banquet from Isaiah 25:6–9 and crafts a story around it. A man invited guests to a feast, but when the time for the meal came and he sent his servant out for the customary call to the banquet, the guests came up with transparently lame excuses why they could not attend. But the host refused to be humiliated and invited townspeople who were not his social equals—those who would never be able to reciprocate by inviting him to a banquet of their own. Still, there's room at the feast even after the outcasts come, so the host invited even more people, strangers from beyond the community. One way or another, he would have his seats filled.

The implications are clear to Jesus's listeners. The messianic banquet is ready. Only those who are invited can attend, and those who do not come have refused the invitation. The result is that the feast draws an unexpected crowd—just as Jesus has.

Having made his point, Jesus delivers a strong message about the cost of following him. Those who come to him must be prepared to give up anything and everything for his sake. Loyalty to him transcends all other attachments. Discipleship is not a decision to be made lightly. In other words, those who follow him must decide which is more important—the banquet or their excuses not to attend.

Discuss

- What costs have you encountered in following Jesus? If someone asked you to explain why following him is worth the cost, how would you respond?

  _____

  _____

  _____

  _____

A CASE STUDY

Imagine: You've just finished reading Luke 12:16–34 about wealth, worry, and seeking first the kingdom, and Jesus appears in front of you as you close your Bible. After your initial shock and a few "I've always wondered about . . ." questions, he makes you an offer: if you're willing, he will completely rearrange your personal budget and daily schedule according to his priorities. He assures you that he will not force his will on you, but you will have to follow through on his decisions if you consent to his offer up front. He assures you that the blessings will be greater than the discomfort.

- Would you accept his offer? Would you tend to experience more fear or relief in turning your budget and schedule over to him? Why?
- In what ways would you expect your money and time to be used differently if Jesus planned everything out for you? Would your life be much different than it is now?
- To what degree do you think this offer is a real option for us today? How specifically do you think God will guide us in our decisions about how to use money and time?

Kingdom Virtues

LUKE 15–18

Years after Jesus ascended, Paul stood up among a group of philosophers and essentially told them that their statue "to an unknown god" was no longer necessary. We know who God is, Paul explained, and he went on to tell them about Jesus. The Athenians didn't buy it—they couldn't get past the absurdity of someone rising from the dead. But Paul's point was profound: God has given us a picture of himself by sending his Son into our midst.

That's what Hebrews says about Jesus too: "The Son is the radiance of God's glory and the exact representation of his being" (Heb. 1:3). If we really want to know what God is like, all we need to do is look at Jesus. He's the exact image of his

Father. The visible expression of the invisible Lord (Col. 1:15). God in the flesh.

So what is God like? Jesus not only shows us, he tells us. He's the kind of God who cares more about mercy than judgment and who is drawn to attitudes like gratitude and humility. It's true that God is majestic and holy and beyond our ability to grasp. But he's also kind and compassionate. He relentlessly seeks those who are lost and helps those who need him. He heals those who are sick and delivers those who are captive. He meets us where we are.

Jesus not only portrays an accurate picture of God; he also portrays an accurate picture of how God's people are supposed to live. The attitudes of the Son are a model for the attitudes of a disciple. When God reveals what he is like, it's more than interesting information. It's an invitation to be like him.

Through dramatic parables and events, Jesus emphasizes the character, values, and attitudes that please the Father. Among them are mercy, gratitude, and humility. Many people follow Jesus, but those who demonstrate mercy, express gratitude, and have a humble perspective of themselves are closest to his heart. He draws near to those who approach him on these terms.

Mercy: Luke 15

Focus: Luke 15:11–32

In response to Pharisaical muttering about the unsavory characters around Jesus— apparently he socializes and shares meals with a lot of unclean people—Jesus tells a cluster of three parables about finding those who are lost. In the first, a shepherd leaves ninety-nine sheep behind to find a single lost one; and in the second, a woman relentlessly seeks a lost coin. Both cases call for a celebration.

The third in this group of parables is one of Jesus's best-known stories. A son requests his share of his father's estate while the father is still living—a shocking insult that effectively declares the son's wish that his father was already dead. Even more shocking is the father's response. He grants the request and, because a sale and division of property is community business, exposes the family to public shame. The son then moves away and squanders his entire inheritance among Gentiles—a disgraceful act that, in Jesus's day, is punishable by a community-wide cutting-off ceremony.

Finally, when he is desperately drained of resources, the son realizes his predicament and decides to return to the father as a hired servant because he knows he will not be welcomed as a son. But the father sees his son from a distance and completely defies expectations again. He runs—something a traditional Middle Easterner never does in public—and reconciles with his son without even requiring an explanation. The father willingly takes the humiliation of the situation upon himself—it's the only way to keep his son from being a village outcast. With the reconciliation complete, the son can be integrated back into the community. The father throws a party to celebrate. There is no punishment, no shunning, no restitution; just a party.

When the older son hears that his brother has been reconciled without a "trial" for his offenses, he's furious. He demonstrates his anger by refusing to join the celebration—a public insult that further shames the family. Once again, the father does the unexpected. He seeks reconciliation with the older son. He pleads with him to accept the prodigal and enjoy the feast. The story ends before the son makes his decision. The answer is left up to the audience.

That's why Jesus eats with "sinners," and the Pharisees are left to think about their response. Will they embrace the completely unmerited grace offered by Jesus? Or will they demand a certain response from the "sinners" before accepting them?

Discuss

- What do Christians today require of "sinners" before we fully accept them into the community of faith? Does our mercy reflect God's accurately? Why or why not?

_____

_____

_____

_____

Gratitude: Luke 16–17

Focus: Luke 17:11–19

As Jesus travels toward Jerusalem, a group of lepers—outcasts from the nearby village—shout to him. They keep their distance

PARADOXES

Jesus often spoke in paradoxes: "there are those who are last who will be first, and first who will be last" (13:30); "whoever tries to keep his life will lose it, and whoever loses his life will preserve it" (17:33); "everyone who exalts himself will be humbled, and he who humbles himself will be exalted" (18:14); "the greatest among you should be like the youngest, and the one who rules like the one who serves" (22:26); and so on. These paradoxes are a dramatic way of demonstrating that God uses a different measuring stick than human beings do; his value system is radically different than ours. As Jesus pointedly told the Pharisees, "what is highly valued among men is detestable in God's sight" (16:15).

in order not to defile anyone, but they come close enough to make their desperation known. If they are ever going to be cleansed and integrated back into the community, it will have to come from the hand of a miracle worker. And because of Jesus's reputation for cleansing lepers, they have hope. This could be their day.

Jesus hears their plea and tells them to go show themselves to the priest—something a leper can do only after he or she has been healed. As they go, they realize that they are in fact cleansed of their disease. And one—only one out of ten—turns back to give thanks.

Once again, the hero of this story is a Samaritan. But this time the Samaritan isn't a character in a parable; he's a real-life outcast, loathed by Jews, who understands the gift he has been given and appreciates the one who has given it. Again, the unexpected takes center stage.

UNEXPECTED PICTURES OF GOD

More than any other Gospel writer, Luke reports Jesus's unexpected metaphors for God. In parables about prayer, the "God" role is played by a sleepy neighbor (11:5–8) and an unjust judge (18:1–8). In other parables, God is represented by a master who commends a dishonest manager (16:1–9) and a king who kills his opponents (19:11–27). He is also pictured as a woman who lost a coin (15:8–10) and a culturally inappropriate father (15:11–32). In each case, the point is not to make a thorough doctrinal statement about God but, either by contrast or comparison with human beings, to highlight an aspect of his nature. These metaphors also had a specific narrative/literary intent: to shock Jesus's listeners with absurd or unexpected pictures, to command their interest and attention, and to help them remember what they had heard.

Discuss

- Do you think some people are more naturally grateful than others? Why or why not? What effects do you think gratitude has on a person's life?

  _____

  _____

  _____

  _____

Humility: Luke 18

Focus: Luke 18:1–14

Jesus tells a parable to show the disciples "that they should always pray and not give up" (18:1). A widow—a woman in a man's world, poor and completely without means of support—had an adversary making demands on her. She had no status for bringing her case to a judge; the wealthy and influential get hearings much more readily. And the particular judge in this story would hear no appeal, would not even be swayed by a sense of righteousness, duty, or devotion to God. He was unjust and without conscience. This widow was, from all outward appearances, in a hopeless situation. Yet she was heard, and her case was resolved. Why? Because she persisted. She made enough noise and outlasted the patience of the judge.

If an unrighteous judge will eventually resolve a case he has no interest in, will not God answer the prayers of his children who cry to him for justice? Won't the compassionate Father be much more willing to hear the petitions of those who call on him? The answer is clear. Of course he will. He responds to those who have faith.

Jesus also tells a parable to those "who were confident of their own righteousness" (18:9). The scene is the morning or afternoon sacrifices at the temple, the only time when Pharisees and tax collectors might be seen praying in the same place. It was customary for a Pharisee to stand somewhat apart from those gathered (so he would not be defiled by them) and to pray out loud. A certain Pharisee thanked God that he was not like other people; he was grateful for his privileged status and superior standing before God, and apparently he wanted those around him to know it. But a tax collector (also apart from the crowd, but not for the same reasons) pleaded for God to have mercy on him. He knew his condition. He beat on his chest— an expression of extreme sorrow seen in the New Testament only here and at the cross (23:48)—and could not lift his eyes to heaven.

"Who went home justified?" Jesus asks. The tax collector. The outcast. The sinner. The one least likely to experience God's pleasure. The one who understood the sacrifice of atonement taking place before him as he prayed. The unexpected recipient of mercy.

Discuss

- Why do you think God answers the humble and hopeless more readily than those who "have it all together"? What other characteristics do you think God is drawn to in his people?

A Case Study

Imagine: A certain pastor in your town is known for preaching pretty good sermons but also for spending most of his time among questionable characters. He hangs out on street corners with addicts and homeless people—a justifiable ministry, to a point. But he also spends a lot of time at places few Christians would go without being embarrassed. More than that, he seems to enjoy hanging out with non-churchgoers much more than he enjoys being with the people in his own congregation. And though he brings many of his "friends" to church, they never quite seem to fit in. Some of his church members have even wondered if he's in the right profession. He doesn't dress the part, talk the part, or act the part of a full-time minister. He seems at home in Sunday morning services, but he's around secular influences the rest of the week.

- To what degree would you view this pastor as "secular," "unspiritual," or "un-Christlike"?

- From this limited information, is it possible that he's discontent with his profession and not very spiritually mature? Is it possible that he's doing exactly what God wants him to do? What signs or evidence would enable you to discern the difference?

- How would you feel if you were a member of this pastor's church? Would you encourage his outward-focused ministry or feel that he is neglecting his own congregation? Why?

Days of Decision

LUKE 19–21

It seemed impossible. Princess Aurora lay in a tower, asleep under a curse, awaiting true love's kiss. But her true love, Prince Phillip, was chained in a dungeon far away at Forbidden Mountain, and an evil witch named Maleficent diligently, zealously watched over her plan to make sure the lips of prince and princess would never meet.

We know the outcome, of course. Fairy tales never end with the prince in the dungeon and the princess under a curse. With the help of some persistent fairies, Phillip escaped, overcame every obstacle Maleficent put in his way, overcame Maleficent herself in the form of a fire-breathing dragon, and found Aurora. It was a dangerous, life-or-death rescue requiring all the courage and stamina he could muster, but no one thinks twice about such risky endeavors when true love is at stake.

The princess has to be saved at any cost. Whatever it takes, the sleeping beauty has to wake up.

We love a good rescue, especially one motivated by love. That's one reason the story of God's life-and-death mission to save us is so compelling. Jesus came into this world "to seek and to save what was lost" (19:10), and it cost him a lot to do so. He fought snakes and scorpions, overcame obstacles and opponents, defied brutal resistance, and lay down his own life in order to rescue those he loves. In God's estimation, we had to be saved at any cost.

In the days leading up to the crucifixion, Jesus continued to demonstrate his rescue mission. Like the characters in his parables—a good shepherd who lost a sheep, a persistent woman who lost a coin, and a father who lost a son—Jesus went after a tax collector and brought him into the kingdom. He taught crowds and warned them of trials to come. He rode into Jerusalem as an unassuming Savior, a King in servant's clothes, and prepared to pay the ultimate price to rescue those he loved.

Seeking and Saving: Luke 19

Focus: Luke 19:1–10

Plenty of people would love to dine with Jesus this day in Jericho, but the Master invites himself to the home of one of Israel's greedy traitors: a tax collector. The diminutive Zacchaeus had climbed a tree to get a glimpse of Jesus as he passed by, and Jesus notices. He calls the tax collector by name and declares that he must stay in Zacchaeus's house. And one of Jericho's least respected citizens couldn't be more pleased.

This, of course, grates against the sensibilities of the crowd. Jesus is in high demand, yet he honors a pariah like Zacchaeus with his attention. But his choice is vindicated when the tax collector repents of his greed. He vows to give half of his possessions

to the poor, and from the remainder he will pay fourfold restitution to those whom he has cheated—well beyond what the
law requires of thieves. Only a few verses earlier, perhaps even
that same day, a rich young ruler could not bring himself to part
with his wealth (18:18–25). Now a much less respectable seeker
detaches himself from his wealth and enters the kingdom with
joy. And, in case anyone missed the point, Jesus emphatically
justifies his visit to the "sinner's" house—"the Son of Man came
to seek and to save what was lost" (19:10).

This theme of seeking and saving the lost is strong throughout
Jesus's ministry, especially as recorded by Luke. In 5:31, it wasn't
the healthy who needed a doctor but the sick. In chapter 15,
shepherds seek lost sheep, housewives turn their homes upside
down to find lost coins, and good fathers go to great lengths to
rescue their lost sons. This is why Jesus came; the incarnation
is a divine rescue mission.

Discuss

- Why do you think Zacchaeus was so zealous about reliev-
  ing himself of his wealth?

  _____

  _____

  _____

  _____

- Do you think restitution is a necessary part of repentance?
  Why or why not?

  _____

  _____

  _____

  _____

BETTER THAN FICTION

Jesus's parable of the minas in Luke 19 is similar to the parable of the talents in Matthew 25, but there are a few significant differences. One is the description of the master. In Matthew, he's simply a man who went on a journey. In Luke, he's a man of noble birth who went to have himself appointed king, and a delegation from the home country followed him to protest his potential appointment. When he does return as king, he has his opponents slain before his eyes. This accurately describes the circumstances around the Roman appointment of Herod as king of Judea in 40 BC and the appointment of Herod's son, Archelaus, in 4 BC. Luke implies that this parable is told at Zacchaeus's house—a man who likely owed his career to Herodian government. But in the parable, the newly appointed king is God (or Jesus as his representative) and, in contrast to Herod and Archelaus, his retribution is against the unrighteous who hoard resources. It would be pure speculation to say this parable was behind Zacchaeus's zealous repentance, but it certainly may have helped motivate the tax collector to get on the good side of the coming King.

The Coming King: Luke 20

Focus: Luke 20:9–18

It's the beginning of the end of Jesus's earthly ministry. With messianic symbolism, he has ridden a donkey into Jerusalem to the praises of the people. He again laments over Jerusalem. On seeing the city this time, he utters an ominous prophecy of its destruction. Why? Because its people "did not recognize the time of God's coming" (19:44). And entering the temple area, he overturns the tables of those who were selling sacrifices and calls them robbers.

Tension is now extremely high between Jesus and his adversaries—mostly the religious leadership, since "all the people hung on his words" (19:48). But Jesus does nothing to lessen the tension. He tells a parable that disparages Israel's history and indicts its current leaders. Drawing on the image from Isaiah and other prophets of Israel as God's vineyard, he tells of a vineyard owner who rented out his property to some farmers while he went on a journey. When harvest time came, he sent a servant to collect some of the fruit, but the tenants beat him and sent him away. The owner kept sending servants, and the tenants kept rejecting them. Finally, the owner sent his own son, assuming that the family connection would demand at least some respect. But no, the tenants killed the son. When the owner returns, Jesus says, he will kill those tenants and give the vineyard to someone else.

What does Jesus mean with such harsh words? Just a few verses before this he has prophesied Jerusalem's destruction, and earlier he called it the city that kills its prophets and stones those who are sent to it (13:34). We know he doesn't mean that Israel will forever be rejected—the rest of Scripture makes it clear that God is not done with his chosen nation and that a time for its fulfillment will come. And Jesus says nothing against the vineyard itself but rather against its stewards—its leadership. But we also know that he doesn't mean that only the generation of religious

THE HUMBLE MESSIAH

Jesus's entry into Jerusalem on a colt—the offspring of a donkey, not a horse, according to Matthew 21:2—was more than a statement of humility. It was a clear claim to be the Messiah. For one thing, it paralleled Solomon's entry into Jerusalem on David's mule for his coronation (1 Kings 1:32–40). More importantly, it fulfilled the well-known prophecy of Zechariah 9:9: "See, your king comes to you, righteous and having salvation, gentle and riding on a donkey, on a colt, the foal of a donkey."

leaders who rejected him will be judged. His parable stretches too far back into Israel's history for that, and the crowd is more resistant than one would expect if this were just an indictment of current leaders (20:16). No, Jesus is prophesying Israel's initial rejection of the Messiah and the gathering of both Jewish and Gentile believers into the kingdom. This vineyard is much bigger, much more inclusive than Israel ever thought.

Discuss

- Why do you think the Pharisees, who knew all of the messianic prophecies extremely well, did not recognize Jesus as the Messiah?

  _____

  _____

  _____

  _____

- Do you think it's possible for us to know God's Word extremely well and not recognize God working in our lives? If so, what can we do to make sure we see him?

  _____

  _____

  _____

  _____

The Return of the King: Luke 21

Focus: Luke 21:25–38

One of Jesus's sermons to a group of disciples in Jerusalem is foreboding—and hard to decipher. Much of it points to the coming judgment on Jerusalem that will take place nearly four decades after his death and resurrection. The city will be surrounded, believers will flee, and the Roman army's destruction will devastate the city, the temple, and the people. But much of his message seems to point to greater, more cataclysmic, more ultimate events. He will return, not only to judge but to redeem. Regardless of how one interprets his words, key points come through very clearly. For one thing, Jesus is the Lord of history, and he will reign when he returns. And those who believe in him should always watch expectantly for his return. We are to be alert, aware of the times, and ready for his coming—in spite of persecution, in spite of the long wait, in spite of any distraction. We are to watch and pray.

Discuss

- What do you think Jesus means by being "ready" for his return? What kind of attitudes, actions, lifestyle, relationships, priorities, and so forth, does a person who is "ready" display?

  _____
  _____
  _____
  _____

CASE STUDY

Imagine: You've spent years preparing for the job of your dreams at a certain organization, but the application process for this position is unlike any other. Long ago, when you first inquired about the position, you were told that nothing was currently open but to wait and be ready. When a position did open up, you would be given a variety of tests to gauge your skills and aptitude. So you waited, studied diligently, and focused on hardly anything else—often to the neglect of your own needs and the needs of those around you.

One day, you receive a call from the organization telling you that your application has been denied. You explain that there must be some mistake; you were never even given the tests. The caller informs you that the organization had placed people around you over the last couple of years to assess how you approach real-life situations. While your knowledge of the career field is to be commended, your values and character, as evidenced by your relationships and attitudes, aren't a good fit for the company. You were tested without knowing it, and you came up short.

- In what ways does this hypothetical situation compare with the religious leaders who couldn't recognize the kingdom of God when it came to them in Jesus? What aspects of God's Word did the leaders focus on? In which areas did they fall short?

- Do you think you and the Christians you know have any pet emphases or perspectives from Scripture that might cause you to miss what God is doing in your life in the moment? If so, what are they?

- How might this example apply to our preparation for Jesus's return? What aspects of his coming—including the mission and ministry that precede it—should we focus on and choose not to focus on?

Mission Fulfilled

LUKE 22–24

"Promises and pie crusts are made to be broken." So said Jonathan Swift, voicing the understandable cynicism we have toward even the best of human intentions. We want to trust people to keep their word, but we know how fickle the heart can be. Promises are easily made and just as easily forgotten.

But God's heart isn't fickle, and his promises aren't weak. He doesn't change his mind like human beings do, and he doesn't lack foresight. When he gives his word, he keeps it, even when that word was given centuries earlier. The long-awaited salvation promised from the earliest pages of Scripture, a promise repeated and expanded in the law and the prophets, is finally accomplished at the cross. God deals with sin by the costliest sacrifice imaginable.

The fulfillment of God's plan is one of Luke's strongest themes. The prophecies of chapters 1 and 2 prove true. Jesus's death and resurrection fulfill terms of the Old Testament covenant. Luke 24 verses 27 and 44 are major statements about God's foresight and faithfulness. At the Last Supper, Jesus establishes "a new covenant" with his disciples that the prophets had foretold. The Gospel concludes with his promise to clothe the disciples with "power from on high." Throughout the ministry of Jesus, God's commitment to his Word is clear. He has sent his Son to accomplish plans that were laid before the foundation of the world.

God's promises are true in our lives too. Jesus commits, among other things, to forgive the sins of those who believe in him, to give his followers authority over evil, to answer prayer, to be with us forever, and to come again in power. These are not the words of a human being with a shaky track record. They are not commitments uttered casually or without foresight. They are rock-solid assurances from a God who cannot lie. Swift's cynicism toward human promises was perhaps justified, but God's Word is another story. In any situation in life, we can count on him to do what he said he would do.

A New Covenant: Luke 22

Focus: Luke 22:14–30

Meals are an important theme in Luke. Jesus has feasted with Levi, with Simon the Pharisee, with another unnamed Pharisee, and presumably with Zacchaeus, and considerable controversy was stirred at each meal. He has told parables of wedding banquets, a "great banquet," and a festive celebration for the return of a prodigal. Before the Gospel ends, he will eat a meal with some disciples along the Emmaus road and reveal his resurrection to them. But the meal he is about to eat in preparation for Passover has a special significance.

Like the procession into Jerusalem on a donkey, this meal is understated. Nevertheless, it's a huge kingdom event. It's the last meal Jesus will have with his disciples before he is crucified, and it symbolizes the life he has lived for them—and will continue to

JESUS'S NAZIRITE VOW?

When Jesus said, "I tell you, I will not eat it again until it finds fulfillment in the kingdom of God" (22:16) and "I tell you I will not drink again of the fruit of the vine until the kingdom of God comes" (22:18), he was using the language of a vow. Nazirite vows were made by declaring the terms and the ending date of the period of dedication, exactly as Jesus did at the Last Supper. If these words do constitute a vow, they may explain in part why Jesus refused to drink the mixture of wine he was offered as he was being crucified (Matt. 27:34). It would have violated his commitment not to drink "the fruit of the vine" until the kingdom comes.

live *in* them—and the blood sacrifice he will soon offer for them. It's a new covenant, built on the old covenant between God and his people but qualitatively different from that relationship.

Much earlier in his ministry, Jesus told a parable of a master who returns from a wedding banquet and, in a stunning reversal of roles, serves the very servants who have been waiting expectantly to attend him (12:35–37). The kingdom is full of contrasts like that: the wisdom of unsophisticated fools, the life that comes out of death, the greatness of service. Now Jesus applies this parable specifically to his own disciples. He is among them "as one who serves" because they have stood by him in his night of trials (22:27–28). Because they have remained—and in spite of the fact that most of them will flee at some point in the next few hours—he confers on them his kingdom. They will eat and drink a much more festive meal at his table in the kingdom.

Discuss

- In what ways have you sought to be "great"—to elevate your position, your status, or your comfort level? Practically speaking, what would change in your life if you adopted Jesus's strategy for greatness?

_____

_____

_____

Moment of Truth: Luke 23

Focus: Luke 23:26–43

By the next day, most of the disciples have scattered. They had trouble staying awake while Jesus prayed desperately in Gethsemane; and Satan has sifted Peter "like wheat," and the strong disciple crumbled. Now, though crowds are watching the convict carry his cross, only some women are truly following him. "Do not weep for me," Jesus says, warning them of the coming judgment against Jerusalem.

As Jesus hangs on the cross, two criminals are executed, one on either side of him. It's a living parable, a graphic depiction of how one comes into the kingdom. According to Matthew and Mark, both criminals hurl insults at Jesus, just as the rest of the crowd does. But Luke tells us something the other Gospel writers neglect to mention: one of the thieves has a change of heart. He rebukes the other thief for slandering a righteous man and asks to join Jesus in the future resurrection. Jesus gives him more than that—he assures the man that his faith, though voiced at the last minute and under duress, will allow him to enter paradise this very day. There will be no demonstration of repentance or fruitful ministry after this conversion. For a man who lived an unrighteous life and is suffering a humiliating death, this is the ultimate picture of grace.

As Jesus dies, the sun darkens, the curtain of the temple is torn in two, and he utters a line from a common bedtime prayer

(Ps. 31:5). A soldier realizes the injustice just committed, many in the crowd mourn, and a devout and sympathetic member of the Sanhedrin named Joseph donates a tomb. The Galilean women who still follow Jesus note the location of the tomb and see it being sealed.

Discuss

- Which of the following characters do you think you would most likely have been if you were present on the day of Jesus's crucifixion: a disciple who fled; a mocker; a woman who followed and mourned; a curious bystander; a thief on a cross; a dissenting member of the court? Why?

  _____

  _____

  _____

- Do you trust deathbed conversions like the one expressed by the thief on the cross? Why or why not?

  _____

  _____

  _____

Luke 24

Focus: Luke 24:13–35

Two disciples are walking from Jerusalem to nearby Emmaus on the day of resurrection when they are joined by a fellow traveler. The visitor asks what they are talking about and, of course, the hot topic was the death of the would-be Messiah and the disappearance of his body earlier that morning. Remarkably, the traveler doesn't dismiss the idea of a resurrection. In fact, he

A COSTLY GIFT

Joseph of Arimathea was a member of the Sanhedrin who had not consented to the council's decision to push for Jesus's execution. Whether he and his family already owned the tomb near the crucifixion site or bought it in anticipation of Jesus's death isn't clear. Either way, donating the tomb for Jesus's use was a generous gesture. It was also costly in at least two other ways: (1) his discipleship would no longer be secret, likely reducing his reputation and influence on the council; and (2) by handling Jesus's dead body, he (along with Nicodemus, according to John 19:39) became ritually unclean just as Passover began. According to the law, he would be excluded from Israel's festival and have to wait a month to celebrate it.

explains how all of Scripture—from the law of Moses through the prophetic books—points to the Messiah's suffering and glorification. Their hearts burn as he is speaking; he seems to make sense of mysterious prophecies that even the scribes have never fully understood. When they arrive at Emmaus, they entreat the traveler to join them for a meal. As he blesses the meal and breaks bread, their eyes are opened to see who he really is, and then he vanishes. They immediately return to Jerusalem—a distance of at least seven miles—to tell the others.

Jesus appears many more times to his disciples, even showing up that same evening when the men from Emmaus are telling their friends about their encounter. He surprises them by simply appearing in their midst, allows them to touch his very solid body, and eats with them. In other words, as Luke is careful to emphasize, this is no ghostly apparition. The resurrected Jesus remains with them and explains how "everything must be fulfilled." He opens their minds to understand Scriptures that they have known all their lives but never before understood.

And he promises that they will soon have a divine encounter with "power from on high."

Discuss

- Why do you think Jesus didn't reveal himself immediately to the disciples on the Emmaus road? Why was it important first to show how Scripture pointed to him?

_____

_____

_____

A Case Study

Imagine: You're in a small group meeting studying Luke 24:36–49, and Jesus really does show up in your midst. Like the early disciples, you are naturally startled and frightened. But he shows you his hands and his feet, assures you that it's really him, and opens your mind to understand things about the Bible you've never understood before. Then he asks if you have any questions.

- What questions would you ask him? Would they be big-picture questions about life or personal questions about your particular issues and circumstances? What kinds of answers do you most need from him?
- In the few moments between the time he first appeared to you and when he explained why he was there, would you be more likely to assume that he had come to: (1) express his love; (2) explain his truth; or (3) tell you what to do? In other words, do you assume that Jesus's highest priority is to have a relationship with us, give us information, or have us accomplish things? Why?

74

Conclusion

The book of Luke ends where it began: at the temple. That's where Gabriel appeared to Zechariah as the priest carried out his duties, and that's where the disciples assembled to praise God after Jesus ascended to heaven. This is Luke's way of putting an exclamation point on the fact that Jesus fulfilled all that God had spoken through the law and the prophets of old. God has revealed himself through the peculiar, chosen nation of Israel.

Though Luke has emphasized that Jesus is God's work of salvation *through* Israel, he has given his readers ample evidence that salvation comes *for* all nations—and not just all nations, but all kinds of people within those nations. Jesus is salvation for those who are rich and poor, healthy and sick, righteous and sinful, prestigious and outcast. As is often said, the foot of the cross is level ground. Nowhere is this more evident than in Luke's Gospel.

This book is the first installment of a two-part series. The "Theophilus" addressed in 1:3 will later receive a second volume about the history of the early church after Jesus's ascension. The book of Acts will continue many of the same themes that the Gospel explored—the fulfillment of God's plan, the gospel for all kinds of people everywhere, and the power and ministry of the Holy Spirit, among other subjects—and will give us vital information on early Christian history not found in any other source. It will provide evidence that this Jesus of the Gospels continues to live and breathe through his people. His ministry didn't end at the cross. In some respects, that's where it began.

As for Luke's Gospel, what began with wondrous glimpses of hope ends with great joy. There's victory in this story of Jesus, and there's victory in the life of everyone who comes to him. Following him can be a hard road, as both Jesus and Luke make clear, but it's a rewarding path. The Gospels tell us emphatically and enthusiastically that Jesus overcame everything—hostile opposition, disease, deception, sin, storms, deprivation, and even death. And it's an open-ended victory. Anyone—absolutely anyone—can join in.

Leader's Notes

Session 1

Luke 1:26–38, first discussion question. The Christmas story is so familiar that we often read Mary's visitation by Gabriel without understanding the trauma it must have involved. Mary's expectations for her future were completely undone by this event, and her reputation would be questioned by practically everyone—Joseph, Elizabeth, and a few shepherds and wise men notwithstanding—for decades to come. As a later prophecy by Simeon would point out, this responsibility of being the Messiah's mother would one day pierce Mary's soul. But the favor of such a high calling must also have led to an awesome sense of privilege, which Mary clearly acknowledged in her song of praise (1:46–55). Discussing the mixed emotions Mary may have had can help humanize her in the minds of readers today, give us an appreciation for her willingness to serve God, and raise questions of how willingly we serve him ourselves.

Luke 1:26–38, second discussion question. This question has long been debated by theologians, and while most Christians understand the importance of the virgin birth, it apparently wasn't considered essential doctrine by Mark and John, who did not include it in their Gospels. In your discussion, help participants see the significance of Jesus being both fully God and fully man as a Redeemer who bridges the gap between a holy God and sinful humanity.

A Case Study. This scenario is drawn from Mary's experience, but the dynamics are the same in the lives of John the Baptist and Jesus. The principle that God's greatest works involve the greatest sacrifices is evident not only in these examples but in most major characters in the Bible.

Session 2

Luke 4:16–30, discussion question. It may be helpful to point out that during the ministries of Elijah and Elisha, Israel was apostate and under God's judgment. The ministries of these two prophets were essentially a rebuke against corrupt kings and idolatrous practices among the people. By comparing his ministry to these prophets, Jesus was using examples loaded with unflattering implications.

Session 5

Luke 12:13–34, discussion question. Many commentators see Luke as antiwealth because of these negative statements and parables about the rich. (See also Luke 4:18; 6:20, 24; 7:22; 9:3, 25; 14:33; 16:13–15, 19–25; 18:18–27; 19:1–10; 21:1–4.) But even within Luke, wise stewardship is praised (16:1–13), and the generosity of those who have ample resources is commended throughout Luke and Acts. Help participants avoid two errors in this discussion: (1) that somehow poverty is a spiritual virtue in itself and wealth is sinful in itself; and (2) that wealth is a necessary blessing of the gospel. The biblical perspective is that while greed is sinful, using, seeking, and wisely managing wealth for kingdom purposes is commendable.

Session 7

Luke 21:25–38, discussion question. There has been a tension in church history between living for the long haul and living with an eye on Jesus's imminent return. Assuming that the end is near has caused some people to live irresponsibly and avoid solving long-term problems. On the other hand, assuming that the end is far into the distant future has caused some people to settle into the culture and live without any sense of urgency with regard to God's purposes. Relevant questions to this discussion include: Do you plan for tomorrow if you're watching for his return today? To what extent should a Christian be involved in long-term social/political/economic/environmental issues? Do we grow deep roots in society or "pack lightly" for the journey? Is it okay to make long-term investments? And so on. Ultimately the group should be able to arrive at a balance between two extremes.

Session 8

A Case Study, second set of questions. You may get two different sets of answers to these questions. Most Christians know the right answer—that Jesus is primarily interested in having a relationship with us—but then function out of a subconscious assumption that he is more interested in getting us to understand truth or to do the right thing. Obviously, understanding and behavior are aspects of a real relationship, but many believers operate out of a performance-based relationship with God rather than a relationship based on unconditional love and acceptance. As much as possible, let group members explore their deepest expectations about God. Is our gut-level assumption that he wants us to enjoy, to know, or to do? In other words, is the gospel primarily relational, intellectual, or behavioral?

Bibliography

Arnold, Clinton E., ed. *Zondervan Illustrated Bible Backgrounds Commentary.* Grand Rapids: Zondervan, 2002.

Bailey, Kenneth E. *Jacob and the Prodigal: How Jesus Retold Israel's Story.* Downers Grove, IL: InterVarsity Press, 2003.

———. *Jesus Through Middle Eastern Eyes: Cultural Studies in the Gospels.* Downers Grove, IL: InterVarsity Press, 2008.

———. *Poet and Peasant* and *Through Peasant Eyes: A Literary-Cultural Approach to the Parables in Luke.* Combined edition. Grand Rapids: Eerdmans, 1983.

Bock, Darrell L. *Luke.* Downers Grove, IL: InterVarsity Press, 1994.

First Fruits of Zion. *Torah Club.* Vol. 4, *The Gospels and Acts.* Marshfield, MO: First Fruits of Zion, 1994–2004.

Keener, Craig S. *The IVP Bible Background Commentary: New Testament.* Downers Grove, IL: InterVarsity Press, 1993.

Lancaster, D. Thomas. *King of the Jews: Resurrecting the Jewish Jesus.* Littleton, CO: First Fruits of Zion, 2006.

Wright, Tom. *Luke for Everyone.* London: SPCK, 2001.

**WALK
THRU THE
BIBLE®**

Helping people everywhere
live God's Word

For more than three decades, Walk Thru the Bible has created disciple-ship materials and cultivated leadership networks that together are reaching millions of people through live seminars, print publications, audiovisual curricula, and the Internet. Known for innovative methods and high-quality resources, we serve the whole body of Christ across denominational, cultural, and national lines. Through our strong and cooperative international partnerships, we are strategically positioned to address the church's greatest need: developing mature, committed, and spiritually reproducing believers.

Walk Thru the Bible communicates the truths of God's Word in a way that makes the Bible readily accessible to anyone. We are committed to developing user-friendly resources that are Bible centered, of excellent quality, life changing for individuals, and catalytic for churches, ministries, and movements; and we are committed to maintaining our global reach through strategic partnerships while adhering to the highest levels of in-tegrity in all we do.

Walk Thru the Bible partners with the local church worldwide to fulfill its mission, helping people "walk thru" the Bible with greater clarity and understanding. Live seminars and small group curricula are taught in over 45 languages by more than 80,000 people in more than 70 countries, and more than 100 million devotionals have been packaged into daily maga-zines, books, and other publications that reach over five million people each year.

Walk Thru the Bible
4201 North Peachtree Road
Atlanta, GA 30341-1207
770-458-9300
www.walkthru.org